Table of Contents

Chapter 1: Personality Characteristics of Successful Police Officers and some Pitfalls

Cops take charge

Officers often must take charge and do so in a way that is politely assertive and confident at chaotic accidents, crimes in progress, and domestic disturbances. The old adage that cops run towards calamity while every other reasonable person is running from the turmoil is true. Most good cops by nature somewhat outgoing, empathetic, and friendly but do not shy away from taking charge and issuing directions as needed.

People often characterize officers as being "brave." I won't dispute that as many officers do exhibit great bravery in several instances throughout their careers. While I won't dispute it, I will say that every officer I've ever spoken to who was in a tight spot has privately told me they were indeed afraid during the event. They just managed to act despite the fear. Another comment I've heard is that they were on "auto-pilot." That to me indicates they had achieved a level of training that had them able to respond without a great deal of deep thought. If you can't possibly imagine yourself responding to some of the truly chaotic crimes you will encounter at some point in your career, a different job is probably a better choice for you. Don't believe, however, that each and every day you are going into the lion's den. A reasonably assertive person with proper training will have every opportunity to do well in the job.

There has been great emphasis in recent years for officers to work much more closely with the public; to collaborate and find solutions to neighborhood problems together. The emphasis has been so great I believe some very kind and well meaning people have been drawn to the profession thinking they could essentially be community leaders and organizers with a badge. Some department websites only encourage this notion. As mentioned before, however, the fact remains that the majority of the time a uniformed officer is on duty, he or she will be answering calls for service. While being the eyes and ears for a community is a critical trait for a successful officer I encourage the reader to remember that despite efforts to work more harmoniously with the public, police officers must at times deal very assertively with people they encounter. The parolee, drunk, gang member, or drug-addled individual has little regard for your willingness to attend community meetings or coach Police Athletic League events after hours. Some people must be very assertively ordered to take their hands out of their pockets and sit on the curb.

From time to time, these orders may include profanity for emphasis. And, if things take a bad turn, the officer must use reasonable force to compel a criminal to comply with a lawful order.

Please don't misunderstand. In most cities such a stern admonishment or hands-on force compliance is not a daily or even weekly occurrence. When it does happen, though, (and it will-particularly if you're doing your job to stop and legally detain suspicious people) you must have the ability to step up, take charge, and, if need be physically control a non-compliant person.

If you have trouble being assertive, making eye contact, projecting confidence, and don't think you are capable of being hands-on with a suspect, this is not the job for you. You'll jeopardize your safety and that of your fellow officers.

Sometimes candidates who did not fully appreciate this vital part of the job feel the need to continue in police work despite realizing they lack the temperament for this relatively rare but unavoidable part of police work. Be it pride or financial need, they persist in remaining in the profession. These officers tend to be last arriving at hot calls and avoid self-initiated stops of suspected criminals. In short, they become call takers who document (write reports detailing crimes) but are little use in preventing them or coming to the aid of fellow officers. They are cheating the public and letting down themselves and their co-workers. Perhaps perfectly suited for important occupations helping others, they ideally should have learned more about police work before applying.

Cops work independently

Typically, officers begin their shift attending a briefing. They are brought up-to-date on recent criminal acts, asked to look for violators either by name or identifying information and sometimes asked to give particular attention to an on-going aspect in the geographic areas ("beats") which they are assigned. After the briefing, officers load their cars and drive to their beats where they ideally begin self-initiated patrol activities and attend to calls for service as they come in.

While it's true that the majority of calls require at least two officers to respond and officers assist ("cover") one another on some self-initiated activity, the majority of your day you are working independently. Your sergeant is available by radio or phone and will show up on significant calls, but in large part you are working alone. Unlike firefighters, our cousins in public safety, cops do not associate with one another so closely. At the conclusion of a call involving more than one officer, it is customary to spend a few minutes chatting before going back into service. Cops do often meet to exchange information as well, but for a great part of your shift, you'll be solo. That suits most cops just fine but if you're a person who wants to interact with co-workers throughout your workday, this may be problematic.

Cops are empathetic, but can compartmentalize emotions

You will undoubtedly be involved in some very exciting encounters that put you to the test. However, you may find that for every bad guy you apprehend, you'll encounter dozens more victims of crime. Unfortunately, due to no fault of the PD, some of these crimes may never be solved. At such times you need to document fully whatever you can and also be able to project empathy towards the victim of a criminal act. This is true for all reported crimes but particularly so when someone is seriously assaulted physically or sexually, robbed or otherwise in great pain due to criminal victimization. Emotions are raw at numerous non-criminal events you'll be called to. Responding to a suicide is not uncommon and once you are certain the event is a suicide you'll often be the person comforting loved ones of the deceased until other family members arrive. While it's technically the coroner's responsibility to notify next of kin when someone meets their end, for various reasons you may be called upon to attend to that task. Comforting an elderly woman who hit and killed a drunk who stumbled into the roadway between parked cars is a challenge, but giving comfort is something you should not just feel like you have to do, but something you want to do.

Now and then people apply to be police officers thinking they will be primarily crime fighters, when much more of the job has to do with showing empathy to crime victims and negotiating truces in neighborhood disputes. Just as one should not be a police officer if unwilling/unable to face even physical confrontation, no one should get into the job who does not feel a genuine desire to make a difficult situation better for someone. One of the most important things you'll do as a police officer is comfort others.

In addition, what is sometimes very difficult but necessary is compartmentalizing or "turning off" completely natural emotion in order to complete the job at hand. While you may be attending to a SIDS death of an infant or some other seemingly natural cause of death you must also be examining the scene, interviewing witnesses and collecting evidence as indicated to be certain no criminal act has taken place. To do that successfully often means you can't really work at processing the tragedy of the event while on scene and, in fact, you may clear that call only to be immediately dispatched to some mundane event where the reporting party is clearly wrapped up in what seems (especially now) be be wildly inconsequential. These times can be taxing and while the shorthand expression of "suck it up" is sometimes used, for your own mental health you'll need to be able to decompress in a healthy manner on a regular basis. This is not the booklet for that, but I will comment that having someone trustworthy to confide it is vital. Exercise, meditation, religious expression, and counseling are all reasonable outlets to consider. While I'm not judgmental of a cop having a beer or two sometimes after work in a safe environment, such a coping tool is certainly misadvised as a long-term strategy to deal with suppressed emotions.

Some Pitfalls

I've had the pleasure of working with several psychologists during the course of my career. One who impressed me was Dr. Ellen Kirshman. She has a tremendous amount of experience in working with police officers and authored *To Love a Cop*, a book which goes into far greater detail than I will (or certainly could) regarding some psychological riffs associated with this line of work. I encourage you and the person you love to read it if you continue this path. Kirshman presents some good ideas in how to deal with common psychological problems associated with police work.

In just a few words I'd like to comment on some psychological risks that are completely manageable but sometimes need addressed.

Cops can become too engrossed in cop culture:

Because cops encounter so many people who are not very fond of them, it's common to fall into the "us against them" mentality. It can seem that only fellow cops understand what it's truly like to be a police officer and, if taken too far, you can begin to compartmentalize the public at large into three roles: cop, victim, or criminal. Cops will sometimes begin to associate almost entirely with other cops in a kind of reinforcing loop, which while sometimes comforting, is a skewed way of looking at the world and may ultimately alienate you from people you love. Maintaining relationships with people who are not involved in law enforcement is one way to avoid this trap.

Cops can feel too self-important:

Everywhere you go, people look at you. In large part, what you tell someone to do they pretty much must do or face consequences. Few people are charged with the responsibility and authority of police officers. Who else can arrest people and book them into jail on their word alone? This can be somewhat heady stuff, especially (in my experience) for young new officers. When you carry this attitude with you after hours, you risk alienating friends and family. Aside from damaging your personal life, this way of thinking can inflate your ego. You may come to think if you give someone a non-lawful order, they must comply just because you are the police. If you're lucky, like I was, your spouse will set you straight early on (God love her). Again, the key is to have someone you trust with the courage to let you know if you're getting a bit full of yourself.

Cops can put stress on the back burner

Again, I won't belabor it but despite all the excitement and satisfaction law enforcement brings it also brings a fair amount of stress. Few people are happy to interact with police, sometimes even victims. Events in the field and internal department politics take their toll, as does shift work and disruptions on your days off or vacation (sometimes ruined due to a subpoena requiring you to testify in one of your cases).

I already mentioned the risk of bottling up normal emotions. I will re-state that it is critical to find healthy ways to manage this inevitable byproduct of policing.

I hope I have not unnecessarily discouraged you but I found all the aforementioned to be true. If you have the right temperament, though, all the negatives are manageable and no job is immune to some discomfort. The positives of doing such a meaningful job, though, are tremendous. It can be an exciting job that offers a comradery that is rare in all but perhaps the military. Your impact will continue long after you've left and you can look back with pride on an honorable career. It can be the best job in the world; one I can guarantee you'll think about with some fondness when you reach that magical retirement date. Now, let's maximize your chances of landing that job.

Chapter 2: Education and Deciding to Attend the Police Academy

If you happen to be reading this in your late teens or early 20s you can do yourself a great favor by obtaining a four year college degree. Most departments in the San Francisco Bay Area require some college education (often 30 units in absolutely anything). And, if you put yourself through a local academy, you will often meet the educational requirement. That's all well and good if you want to work 30 years as a patrol officer, and I've had the honor of knowing several officers who were great at their jobs and did just that. Perhaps no person has more impact in a police department than the officer who answers calls for service.

If, however, you think there is ever a chance you'll want to be promoted (and most career officers at one point or another do test for advancement) a college degree will either be required or "highly desirable". Virtually every police chief has at least a BA/BS and many have a master's degree. It's something you should strongly consider.

Some applicants decide they will go to college while working as a cop and it can indeed be done. It's quite a challenge, though, due to long hours, fatigue, and unexpected subpoenas. If you can possibly get that degree before you start, you're way ahead of the game.

Also, please don't automatically pick administration of justice, political science, or criminology. They won't necessarily give you the leg up and if you ultimately decide not to become a police officer there is not much demand for those majors outside of police work. Many attorneys began as cops, and to this day political science is a popular major among aspiring attorneys. Sadly, many people fail the police academy due to incredibly poor report writing skills, so picking a major that trains you to write will be helpful to you as a police officer. Not only that, but being a decent writer will more easily translate to another job outside of police work should you decide that this isn't the path for you. Finally, pick something you're truly interested in.

Putting Yourself Through The Academy

Ideally, you'll want to be hired as an entry-level officer. In doing so, they pay you a full salary while paying your way through the academy. Depending on how far away the academy is from your home, they may also provide lodging for the approximate six months it takes to complete the academy.

While presently there are departments who will hire you as an entry-level officer, a considerable number of departments will require that applicants have already completed the academy or are already employed with a different department (often called "laterals.")

Entry-level positions are difficult to land and often go to people who the departments feel more closely mirror the public they serve.

If you want to increase your chances of being hired by completing the academy in advance, you should know it runs almost six months and currently costs (in the San Francisco Bay Area) approximately $3,500. The academy is full-time with some night exercises. Before you can pay them to enroll, you must complete a basic finger print check, pass a written test, and run the obstacle course.

Before enrolling, be brutally honest with yourself. Can you easily write a couple pages of text with few errors? How's your background? Even If you have misdemeanor crimes of violence, recent drug arrests, or previous employers that may tell background investigators terrible things about you, investing the money and time might lead to bitter disappointment. Give it some thought and don't be afraid to contact an agency to speak to someone involved in hiring. If you are completely frank with them about your background they will probably give you a sense of how that would be perceived by their department. If you feel confident about these things, have the money, and six months time you'll be in a much better position to be hired than an entry-level applicant.

By completing the police academy, you carved six months off the time it takes to have you street ready. Completion of the academy means you can immediately begin the Field Training Program after your background, psychological and medical examinations are complete. Once hired, they may also start you at a higher wage. For many, it's a good move but you need to evaluate risk vs. benefit very carefully.

Where do you want to work?

I was amused more than once when job applicants patiently explained to me they did not want to work as patrol officers; they wanted to be detectives. Of course in every department I've even known, everyone starts as a uniformed patrol officer and some were ultimately assigned the detective position after several years of good work in patrol. I've had other people (who I had a bit more sympathy for) say they wanted to work for our organization because they we were hiring and they simply applied to everyone in the area who was accepting applications. I understood those applicants but you want to do your best to at least narrow your search to somewhere where you'd be happy for at least five years. After that period of time your employer probably won't resent you changing jobs and you're not so entrenched you won't be able to start a new career elsewhere. But going somewhere just because they are hiring may be a very ill fit for you and the agency.

What do you want to do?

If you want to be in the gritty city were there is a high crime activity level and a great deal of potential movement due to the size of the agency then you might consider Oakland, San Jose or further out, Sacramento or Los Angeles. I've had contact with officers in all these departments and some truly love it. You might be one of them. At the other extreme, there are departments were crime is fairly rare and you have a lot of uncommitted time. You also gain experience at a much slower rate. In the San Francisco Bay Area, Atherton, Belmont, Hillsborough, Foster City, and Pleasanton might be towns to consider. I was interested in a mix. I wanted a decent crime rate to remain interested and develop my policing skills but I did not want calls to stack up so far that self-initiated activity (or a coffee break with my pals) was out of the question. Redwood City was perfect for that. I know officers in San Mateo, Daly City, and Fremont that have had similar experiences. By the way, in those big cities I mentioned they also have places with a lower crime rate but officers are typically started (appropriately so) in hot spots.

Finally, in local law enforcement you may also consider Sheriff's Offices. Some are excellent (I've had nothing but good dealings with the San Mateo County Sheriff's Office as well as Santa Clara County SO) with the only downside I can see is the fact you'll have to work the jails for a period of time.

Personally, I found the jails unpleasant. They were places I deposited criminals. On the up side, sometimes an SO will take a chance on someone knowing they can try them out in the jail. If they do well, the SOs have quite a few positions you can pick from if you do a good job, so your opportunities increase. Additionally, in the event you kind of run out of gas towards the end of your career, you can be a bailiff or work in transportation and end your career in an honorable manner without running from call to call.

Finally, where you pick to work will maximize the chances you end up doing the kind of police work you like- but there are no assurances. Newton, Connecticut is an affluent community with a low crime rate of approximately 25,000 people, but officers in that relatively small police department were pressed into one of the highest stress calls imaginable. There are beats in Los Angeles where officers patrol areas with few calls for service. In whatever type of city or town you work in, when the bell rings, you'll be expected to answer.

Chapter 3: What to Expect of the Application and Testing Process
Testing Process

While I hope you read this whole thing, I understand if you just jumped to the important part. After all, you want to be hired as a police officer and perhaps you have no interest whatsoever in what in my pontifications. That's fair. After all, you bought the booklet.

Though most of my background has to do with the San Francisco Bay Area, I'm certain some of these tips will help you out wherever you apply. Give this some thought, do your homework, put in a bit of practice, and you'll be in good shape.

Many departments will require you to pass a written examination and physical agility test before they allow you to participate in the interview process. These can vary considerably and a quick web search or phone call will tell you exactly what is required depending on what your agency demands. Most agencies use a written test distributed by Police Officers Standards and Training, or POST. It is essentially an English comprehension test as there is no expectation at this point that you are familiar with criminal law. The test is primarily multiple-choice and fill in the blank. There is a minimum score to pass and you can review samples on the POST website.

 A common physical agility exam might involve a 500-yard run, and obstacle course, a 165-pound dummy drag, and making your way over both a chain link and solid wood fence. This test is commonly held at a local police academy.

If you did fine in high school and did reasonably well in the minimum amount of college required, the written test should not be very taxing. Still, if you've been out of school for awhile it would be a good idea to refresh your test taking skills by taking the practice tests offered by POST, as well as perhaps buying one of the soft cover books that give you an opportunity to take several practice tests and an answer key to judge how you're doing. Multiple-choice tests in many respects are essentially true/false tests as a test taker with a bit of skill can usually quickly dismiss two of four choices in a multiple-choice examination.

If you're reasonably physically fit, you should have no problem with the physical test. Most academies allow you to practice once or twice before test day; you should take advantage of that even if you're fit. Men and especially women sometimes have trouble with the wall, and if you think that may be a problem you'll want to work on assisted pull-ups and a technique for climbing that thing. Keep in mind that when you're chasing a bad guy you'll have about 30 extra pounds of gear on you, so don't just work on making it over the wall; work on making it over with gusto.

A general comment about fitness. The days of obese, smoking, donut-eating cops are not entirely over, but they are on the wane. At least that's true in the San Francisco Bay Area. By the time I left, most of the cops I worked with were fit and only one or two smoked. Your confidence level in physical confrontations is directly tied to your fitness level, and your chances of using what someone might see as excessive force increases greatly if you feel completely outmatched, out of breath, and out of strength. What could just be a wrestling match until the Calvary arrives might turn into something more disconcerting if you don't keep up with your fitness.

Written Application

These days it's kind of hard to mess this part up. Almost always online, as long as you can type (or know someone who can) you have no excuse whatsoever not to submit a clearly written application. This will come up more than once as you're applying to be a police officer but, no matter what, tell the truth. There are legitimate and reasonable reasons why you may, let's say, have been terminated from a job. Not including that information because you're hoping no one is the wiser? You may as well not even fill the application out. You'll be submitting proof of passing the written and physical exam in order for your application to be accepted.

Homework Moving Forward

You're applying for a career. In the bay area, you'll earn approximately $100,000 a year in salary and overtime within your first few years. Perhaps because it's civil service and so easy to apply I found a startling number of people who were hugely unprepared to participate in even the initial job interview. With countless online resources there is no excuse whatsoever for you to not know a fair amount about the police department you're trying to get hired on to. Read their website and remember some key information – how many people they serve, how many officers work there, what the last few years have looked like for the department, and so on. Some departments publish an annual report, and virtually all have a mission statement that you should be familiar with. Know who their police chief is and research independently to get a bit of information in him/her. Know what programs they are currently involved in.

Make sure you participate in one or two ride alongs. On any department's website it will give instructions on how to go on a ride along, but in the event that they do not, simply call the PD and ask to be connected to the person who schedules ride alongs.

On the ride along the officer will usually be willing to answer your questions and give you some insight you would otherwise not know about the department.

Be on your best behavior, as hiring managers sometimes ask the officer what he thought of the applicant. Departments would not likely proceed with an applicant the officer thought very poorly of. It's perfectly fine to ask the officer why he/she enjoys working there and it may give you some information you can put to good use in your interview. If the officer is unhappy, he or she will likely tell you. It's wise to listen but also keep in mind it's difficult to judge an entire department based on the views of a single officer.

Chapter 4: Next Steps in Hiring – Interviews and the Physical Exam

The First Interview

The first panel interview you will face will commonly be composed of a sergeant, some officers, perhaps a non-sworn member of the department, (a dispatcher or record clerk) and an HR person. This is to ensure everyone is asked the same questions and that you are not asked anything regarding race, gender or sexual orientation. I've personally never seen that happen and once HR feels comfortable with the hiring team they may decide not to attend.

First, and not to insult you, dress the part. Showing up in cheap slacks, your uncle's shirt, and a tie you borrowed from your 80 year-old dad is not going to cut it. Take my advice. Spend a bit on a blue sport coat. Buy a white shirt, some tan slacks, dress shoes, and a solid color tie (navy blue is a safe choice). And, as long as I'm on a rant, have the tie reach the belt. I've interviewed guys with ties that land about four inches above their belly button. I've no clue on women's fashion but something conservative is not a bad idea.

A few hundred dollars will get you a nice suit that you can wear again for the Chief's Oral (as the panel is completely different) and as many court appearances as you like. Add to your wardrobe as you start making some money.

Interview Questions and Guidelines for Answers

I've got a boatload of questions that have been asked on initial interviews. I'm not going to give them to you, though. I still have great respect for the people who do the job and I don't want to give you rote answers that may land you a job you have no business being in. I will, however, give you a general sense of what can be asked and encourage you to answer them as completely as possible. Too many applicants give answers to questions so briefly that really don't give the interviewers a sense of who they are. I'm going to encourage you to leave everything in the room and hope for the best.

Here's some questions I'm almost certain they will ask. They may ask them a bit differently, but the theme will be the same and your answer will be fine regardless of how they ask it.

Why do you want to be a police officer?

There are number versions of this question. You need to prepare for it and rehearse your answer. A word of advice: don't immediately reply, "I want to help people." I've heard that answer so many times I wanted to throw the applicant out the window. Of course you should not want to be a police officer if you did not want to help people but you're going to have to do better than that. My reply (which often stymied applicants) was something like "that's commendable but you can help people by being in health care, by being in medicine, by teaching....what is it about police work that attracts you?"

Here's a better answer that is truthful and allows you to expand on your answer "I think this position will give me a lot of job satisfaction." Then, you expand on that. Do you think you could comfort victims? Would you feel some satisfaction arresting someone who would hurt others? Do you like working largely independently? Does having a different task at hand each day appeal to you? Is working with a team attractive to you? Would you like to have a job you are proud of? The list can go on and on and I encourage you to give it much thought and be ready for this sure to be asked question. You should emphasize any positive experience you have working with the public. No one should do this job without enjoying working with people and mention of your success in this area will be appreciated.

Why this police department?

Here's where you get the benefit of your homework. Be sure to tell them some facts about their PD (even simple stuff like your serve a population of XX and have a sworn force of YY) and that you've talked to others and went on a couple ride alongs and you've been impressed by the professionalism of the department and how welcoming people are. Give them some honest reasons why their department would be a place you would appreciate working for.

Where else have you applied?

This will not be a big problem unless you've applied and widely desperate departments. If the places you've applied to are in the same ballpark, you're fine. If you've applied at Oakland PD and Atherton PD you're in a tough spot. It's not a deal breaker that you've done this but you'll simply have to come clean about wanting to get your foot in the door wherever you can get hired. As long as you're honest and can honestly tell them you'll give them no less than five years you will not certainly be rejected for trying to land virtually any police officer job opening. Don't be surprised, though, if they ask you which of the many places you have applied you would prefer to work. This is tricky because if you rate the place you're interviewing at third or forth you should not expect to proceed to the next step. Of course if that department happens to truly be your first selection, telling them so is just fine. A middle of the road answer (which may certainly be true) is that you'd most like to work for the agency that has the confidence in you to hire you first.

What makes you think you'll do well in this job?

Police officers who are successful have something in common. They all work well with people and, ideally, they work well with people from different backgrounds and are good communicators. Police officers enjoy a challenging job where each day can offer them new experiences. They also consider themselves team players and take satisfaction in solving problems. This is also a moment where you can mention your superior written skills (if that's the case) and your demonstrated ability to work well without close supervision.

What are your strengths?

This is actually a two-part question, because the asking of this question guarantees you'll be asked to name your weaknesses next. Obviously, prepare for both.

If your biggest weaknesses include losing your temper too easily, holding racial stereotypes, or difficulty working with others, stop here and re-think your career choice. Other weaknesses are certainly acceptable, especially if you add what you are doing to improve the weakness. I, for instance, have some of the worst navigation skills of anyone I know. I'm easily lost and have difficulty finding locations. (Imagine my delight when GPS became readily available.) Knowing that, my first order of business upon a department showing interest in me would be to spend a considerable amount of time driving through the town I hoped to be hired by. Indeed, once I was hired I spent a considerable amount of my off duty time devoted to learning the city and that effort was worthwhile because, despite my efforts I still had trouble during my training phase and even afterwards at times finding my way around town.

Scenario Questions

These are questions where you are asked what you would do as an officer if such and such took place. It's not likely you'll be asked any technical legal questions as you're not yet expected to be well versed in the law at this point. The questions tend to lean towards ethical matters or something to get a feel regarding your possession of common sense.

Many ethical questions don't really ask what the right thing to do might be. Rather, they ask if you are willing to do the right thing even when doing so is difficult or make you unpopular with your new co-workers. Those are fair questions and not reporting unethical or illegal actions of co-workers is simply (and truly) unacceptable. Keep that in mind.

Common sense questions sometimes deal with whether you'll use sound judgment despite being lawfully allowed to chose different courses of actions. I, for instance, was asked what I would do when dispatched to a large angry crowd forming for a protest. I'm first to arrive and while evaluating the situation one of the protestors spits in my face. No other officers are yet present. What would I do? They were seeing if I would foolishly exercise my lawful right to arrest the spitter, in spite of the fact I was clearly outnumbered and doing so would jeopardize my safety. My answer was to get a good look at the offender so that when/if law enforcement had things well in hand I could pursue a safe and lawful arrest.

Think the question through a bit. Weigh risks versus benefits in taking certain actions and be prepared to follow up with why you would take the course of action you describe. Don't feel compelled to immediately blurt out an answer.

As mentioned, there are a number of questions you might be asked. If you prepare thoroughly for the basic ones I've described and take your time with questions you may not be expecting, you'll do fine.

The Chief's Oral

If you've made it this far, you've done well enough that you are a serious contender for the position. It's great news. In the sad event you receive a reject letter after your first interview, there is certainly no harm in calling the leader of the interview team (the highest ranking member) and politely ask what you might do to improve your chances next time. Be polite and not defensive and you may learn something very valuable for your next interview wherever that may be.

The term Chief's Oral if often exactly that: you'll often be interviewed by the Chief of Police and usually a command person or two. Some chiefs however, may have command staff personnel conduct the "Chief's Oral." I conducted dozens of them with one or two other Captains, so don't necessarily think you are second tier because the Chief is not present at your interview.

As before, you'll want to dress sharp and arrive about ten to 15 minutes early for your interview. Don't be so distracted by thinking about your upcoming interview to forget to be gracious to the person you meet. That person may well be the Chief's assistant, and the Chief has been known to ask him or her what he/she thinks of the applicant.

Your preparation for the Chief's Oral will be similar to your first interview, as the questions will not differ all that much. Bone up on any answers you struggled with in your initial interview. If you have time to get in another ride along it can't hurt. One question you might be asked in any interview is "what have you done to prepare yourself for this interview?" and being able to say you participated in ride alongs shows a sincere interest in the department, as does rattling off some knowledge you've obtained through your homework.

Don't be surprised if you're asked to write a short essay while you wait. Unfortunately, though you've already taken a test that was intended to measure writing skills there is virtually no multiple-choice test that can accurately measure that skill. You've not been asked to write something to bring with you to the interview because, frankly, they don't want someone helping you with the essay. Having you write two or three paragraphs gives the Chief an idea if you have the writing skills necessary to write reasonably good police reports. Sadly, I can report we've passed on many applicants based on these essays. Not too concerned about spelling in this wonderful age of spell check, if the applicant can not string together a few sentences without grievous grammar errors the chances of them succeeding in a job where each shift may demand a comprehensive police report is very low.

The subject you may be asked to write about can be as basic as describing the last pleasant trip you took or perhaps why you wish to be a police officer. It's not the subject matter or even what you write that will be examined but rather how well you write.

After being introduced to the Chief and command staff present and perhaps a bit of small talk the questioning will begin. Most Chief's will be pleasant and make an effort to put you at ease. The days of the so-called "stress interview" is over and it's very unlikely you'll be asked any scenario questions at this interview.

You've done your homework and you're largely prepared for what the Chief will ask you. When you address the chief you can't go wrong with "sir" or "chief." While he/she can be as informal as he/she likes, you should pay attention to little things like posture (sitting up straight and not crossing your legs can't hurt). A bit of unforced humor will probably be appreciated but should certainly not make up the bulk of your interview.

If the interview is going well you may be asked if there is anything in your background you'd like to reveal and explain before a background investigation is commenced. Be frank. It is the right thing to do, will likely be discovered anyway and you have an opportunity to explain yourself. Some candidates have bad credit scores but a reasonable reason for being in that position. Others have told me they think their ex-husband or wife may have some unkind things to say due to a messy divorce.

Illegal drug usage may come up. There is no universal standard in regards to what the Chief may think is disqualifying. An arrest should have you questioning if you should even apply for the position, as would recent use of any illegal drug with the possible exception of marijuana. In my experience, few applicants report never using any illegal drug with marijuana topping the list. As I mentioned, there is no firm tipping point and different Chiefs have different opinions regarding how much, if any, illegal drug use will disqualify you for further consideration. Be careful with words like "experimentation." I've had candidates tell me they have experimented with marijuana in college but when pressed for how many occasions they "experimented" was met with the answer of thirty or forty times. That exceeds what would be defined as an "experiment" and the candidate would be better served by simply saying he/she had used marijuana during their years at college.

Towards the conclusion of your interview, it is quite common for the Chief to ask if you have any comments. Take advantage of leaving your final best impression before the conclusion of the interview. First, thank the Chief for allowing you to opportunity to interview for the position. Then, summarize briefly why you think you would be a fine addition to the organization. It's here you can touch on your education, experience, and personal qualities that will lend themselves to the position. You can end it with saying something similar to "I'm confident I'd be a good fit for your organization and I won't let you down." If the Chief asks if you have any questions before you leave it's fair to ask when you could expect to hear if you will continue with the process.

The Background Investigation

If the happy event you pass the Chief's interview you'll soon receive a background package. It is essentially asking you to provide a great deal of information to allow the agency to complete a thorough background investigation to determine if they wish to make a hiring offer. This is essentially the final step you have significant control over. While I'll cover the psychological and medical examinations, those only take place if you have "passed" the background and a hiring offer is immanent.

The background investigation starts with a lengthy form asking you to list contact information for immediate family members, current and previous employers, educational institutions and degrees you've obtained, military information if applicable, financial information, etc. Spend some time on this and be as thorough as you can. Incomplete packages will only result in delaying or perhaps even ending your hiring process. After you complete the package be sure to make a photocopy of it in the event you're ever asked to complete another.

Your references should know you're applying for the position and ideally be supportive of your efforts to be hired as a police officer. Every now and then I've seen very thorough investigators ask your references who else may be able to weigh in on your desire to enter law enforcement. Something to think about.

After submitting your package you'll meet a background investigator. Some departments assign their own law enforcement officer to the investigation, while others contract with private firms to complete the background. The investigator will review the contents with you and ask you any further questions he/she may have. While the background investigator technically has no say on whether you are hired or not, he/she can, consciously or not, slant the background in such a way as to make you a more or less qualified candidate. Most of the narratives written by these investigators actually begin recounting their meeting with you noting your dress and demeanor so take the interview seriously. They may meet you at your home for the initial interview or ask you to meet at their office. In either case, dress appropriately. A suit or sport coat is not required but don't meet the investigator at your home in your pajamas or at their office in your gym attire.

Something may come up during the background that requires further contact with the investigator. Be sure to reply promptly, thoroughly, and honestly.

While you cannot change the past, you can give it context. Say, for instance, you were fired from a job while an adolescent for consistently being late. You've had to list that in your package but you can spend a moment with the investigator explaining why you were chronically late. Perhaps you had a good reason or, more likely, you were a bit immature. You can mention that and point out you learned from your poor judgment and other employers were happy to have you work for them. If you've had a painful divorce, you can give them your perspective on why your ex-spouse has bad things to say about you. Be cautious, though, about saying too many negative things about anyone. In short, it makes you look bad. You're hoping to enter an occupation where accountability means a great deal. To attempt to give the appearance that virtually nothing in your background is your fault works against you. Think about it. Even if your spouse was terrible, you minimally showed poor judgment in picking such a person as a life partner. Don't overdo the victim card.

Part of the background that often causes applicants anxiety is the polygraph or "lie detector." I've rarely seen people fail these tests. There is a body of evidence that discounts polygraphs as flawed science at best and a sham at worst. Perhaps President Nixon was right when he said ... "I don't know how accurate they (polygraphs) are, but I know they'll scare the hell out of people." In my experience, when people are tripped up by this part of the process it's because they reveal something they had not previously reported out of fear it will be caught during the examination. They often make these revelations immediately before the process begins. Or, the examiner may say the applicant showed some biological response to a certain question, leading the applicant to blurt out they were less than honest when first asked. The lesson here is to simply tell the truth and not over think it. If the examiner does say you showed a reaction to a question and you have no idea why, say exactly that. If it made you remember a distant event you wish you had remembered to reveal, then report that. A single hiccup (especially on an fairly innocuous question) will not result in you "failing" the polygraph examination. Most polygraph reports I've read actually give themselves some wiggle room by saying a single question resulting in some concern should not lead the employer to disqualify an applicant.

If you "pass" the background you're almost there. All that remains is a psychological assessment and a physical examination. The good news is that very few people fail either of these two final examinations. I'm of the opinion that most people who have the psychological flaws that would exclude them from police work have evidenced inappropriate behavior in their lives that is revealed in the background investigation. The bar for the medical examination is not that high and if you "fail" that, it's probably because you have such a serious medical condition you should make regaining your physical health your priority.

The Psychological Examination

Your psychological examination will almost certainly involve an interview with the psychologist as well as some psychological testing. Psychologists have earned a PhD in psychology and are well versed in interviewing and psychological testing. Psychiatrists are medical doctors who are therefore permitted to prescribe medication but may actually have less knowledge in psychology than psychologists.

First, let me comment that I've never seen a candidate "fail" the psychological exam due to psychopathology (technically, a diseased mind). I've yet to see a candidate get that far in the testing process to be judged suffering from a psychosis. If you "fail" (again, highly unlikely) it will not be because you're "crazy." I'll begin and end this section with a bit of advice: don't over think it. The psychologist cannot read your mind and is not going to probe to find your darkest secret. Above all, be honest. Directly answer the psychologist's questions. There is no need to be defensive. I know every profession has its bad eggs but psychologists in general are good and accepting people. They realize essentially everyone has something they could perhaps improve upon but are not overly judgmental. Be yourself, be forthright. In all likelihood it will be one of the easiest parts of this process.

What to expect in the Psychological Examination

In almost all cases this will be a face-to-face interview. The psychologist will ask questions that give hem/her information about your life situation and personality. The psychologist will likely ask you about your family situation, educational and employment history and a number of questions to get some idea about your intelligence. Don't be surprised if he/she asks about your marriage or significant other, questions regarding how you deal with stress, alcohol or drug usage or other questions that give him an idea of your suitability for being a police officer. The interview will likely last less than an hour and you may leave there actually feeling a bit better. Psychologists have a way of doing that.

Psychological tests

Over the years, a wide variety of psychological tests have been employed to evaluate applicants. IQ tests, projective tests (think of those movies where a shrink gives you a word and asks what first comes to mind. This would also include the famous inkblot or Rorschach test). The Minnesota Multiphasic Personality Inventory (MMPI) has been around for decades and measures a number of personality factors. Last I checked, there are well over five hundred multiple-choice questions in that inventory. Every department picks their own psychologist, but I've found virtually all of them end up with psychologists that perform the face-to-face interview and the MMPI. As I said at the beginning, simply be yourself and answer honestly. While I'm quite certain some psychologists can be scammed, they make their living sizing up people. It would be foolish to put a false face forward when being interviewed by one. In regards to the MMPI you'll probably notice being asked the same question more than once (sometimes worded just a bit differently). For our purposes, that is considered a lie check. Psychologists refer to it as "validity," but it means essentially the same thing. If you're trying to manipulate the test, you may answer the same question differently during those 500 plus questions. This lets the psychologist know you're trying to hook wink him/her and that will not bode well for you. Answer honestly without stewing on the questions too much and you'll be fine.

Physical Exam

At this point, it's all but over. Only serious medical conditions will preclude you from police employment.

I'll mention hesitatingly that you do have some control in regards to being tested for drugs. I hesitate because if you're actively using drugs this is not the job for you. In addition to the health risks, you'll be seizing drugs on a regular basis and if you're tempted to pilfer them you're disgracing the job and committing a felony. Moreover, most drug users are known to other drug users, and if one of them decides to reveal your habit to your employer it will end badly for you. Just so you know, though, the arguably most innocuous of illegal drugs (marijuana) stays in your system the longest. Cocaine and opiates clear you system in a couple days, but if you regularly use marijuana it can be detected up to a month after your last use.

At this writing Washington and Colorado have legalized use of marijuana (though, oddly, not the selling of it just yet). California has all but legalized it because for a hundred dollars you can visit a washed up MD who will "prescribe" it for virtually any malady you state you suffer from. I fully support its use when truly medically warranted but the system seems to have some flaws. Unlike every other prescription I've ever seen it does not come with dosage or frequency of use. You're simply allowed to have and grow it. I'm not sure how this will impact police departments. If you have a "prescription" for marijuana will a department frown on hiring you? I suppose it's completely up to the COP. Since it stays in your system so long, though, I'd be hesitant to hire a cop that would test positive for THC after a shooting or fatal car accident.

Chapter 5: You're Hired! Now What?

Being offered a job after everything you've been through is thrilling. Enjoy the moment; you've earned it. One of two things will happen next. If you've been to the academy, you'll be issued equipment, scheduled to be sworn in, and assigned a Field Training Officer (FTO). You'll be given a start date and you'll of course arrive a bit early and ready to go. Between the offer and start date you can do yourself a favor by working on memorizing the radio codes employed by your department and driving around the city to help you with orientation skills. You'll have plenty to learn and if you can get a jump on those to things you'll be ahead of the game.

Ideally, FTOs are selected because they've demonstrated themselves to be excellent officers and have shown a knack for instructing. Good FTOs see their job as helping to make an applicant successful. Sadly, I've seen FTOs that seemed more intent on washing recruits out of the program. They somehow saw that as a badge of honor. They had no business being an FTO and, fortunately, they were the exception. In any case, if you work 30 years in this job you'll undoubtedly experience a number of different bosses or supervisors. As a recruit officer, your FTO is your first boss and you'll obviously want to please him or her and do your best.

Unless instructed otherwise, you should use your new supervisor's title when addressing him or her. It's "FTO Smith" unless the FTO tells you not to use the title. You want to listen more than talk and be quick to volunteer to do essentially any job that comes your way. As a recruit, you may be dispatched far off your beat to handle a call you have not yet experienced. Even if you have experienced such a call or report the last thing you should do is complain in front of your FTO. You're the new person and as such, unless asked to do anything unethical or illegal, you should do it with a positive attitude to the best of your ability.

Even if you're understandably a little anxious about coming to work those first few weeks it's important to project a positive attitude and a desire to learn more each shift.

If you work in a reasonably active department you'll be amazed by what you'll see in a few short weeks. People who promised to love each other until death beating the snot out of one another, people younger than you so wrapped up into drugs that they're willing to break into houses, or, in the case of females, sell their bodies for a few more hours of escape, parolees who somehow don't understand how lucky they are not to be in prison for the time they were sentenced, drunks that go from wanting to fight to wanting to be pals in a few short minutes, suicide victims and the broken loved ones they left behind, and victims one day only to be suspects the next.

Finally, the crimes in progress where you'll get a description of the offender and some lucky shifts he seems to materialize as if you willed it almost right in front of you and the chase begins. The list goes on and on and it is somehow both sad and exhilarating. You'll find yourself running the shift by in your mind after work, and in the event you found something troubling it's a good idea to talk about it with loved one you trust. Downloading is important. When you've kind of hit your stride during training and you begin looking forward to your next shift, you'll know you picked the right profession.

If you're fortunate, co-workers will welcome you. However, you should not be surprised or disheartened if you are somewhat ignored by the regular cops. It sometimes takes awhile to be accepted into the group. If you do your best and don't impose yourself onto the group prematurely, you'll almost be certainly welcomed after you successfully complete the FTO program. It's very common for the recruit (or "boot") to host a BBQ or buy a round of drinks on the last shift of the FTO program. Don't pass this opportunity up to be formally accepted.

Finally, I'll end with a sentence from the forward: "Remember that your only capital is your character. Therefore, guard it carefully." That continues to be sound advice today. You'll soon establish a reputation. You want it to be a positive one where people know they can rely on you and you're always willing to help a co-worker.

Few traits are as important as honesty for police officers. Your superiors at one time did your job and recognize you're bound to make mistakes and errors in judgment now and then. Don't for a second be tempted to not to lie about an event you are involved in. Even fairly serious misbehavior (if not occurring on a regular basis) will not likely cost you your job. Lying about even minor things will.

With your character intact and a positive attitude you're on your way. Congratulations!

www.ingramcontent.com/pod-product-compliance
Lightning Source LLC
Chambersburg PA
CBHW020519160726
47991CB00007B/3030